$0.02 In Debt

Inner Thoughts Throughout My Great Depression

Danielle Herzner

BookLeaf Publishing
India | USA | UK

Copyright © Danielle Herzner
All Rights Reserved.

This book has been self-published with all reasonable efforts taken to make the material error-free by the author. No part of this book shall be used, reproduced in any manner whatsoever without written permission from the author, except in the case of brief quotations embodied in critical articles and reviews.

The Author of this book is solely responsible and liable for its content including but not limited to the views, representations, descriptions, statements, information, opinions, and references ["Content"]. The Content of this book shall not constitute or be construed or deemed to reflect the opinion or expression of the Publisher or Editor. Neither the Publisher nor Editor endorse or approve the Content of this book or guarantee the reliability, accuracy, or completeness of the Content published herein and do not make any representations or warranties of any kind, express or implied, including but not limited to the implied warranties of merchantability, fitness for a particular purpose.

The Publisher and Editor shall not be liable whatsoever...

Made with ❤ on the BookLeaf Publishing Platform
www.bookleafpub.in
www.bookleafpub.com

Dedication

The few who read this are probably the same who inspired it.
Thank you for accepting, tolerating, helping, forgiving, remembering, and loving me.
You're forever in my heart

Preface

2025 is my thirty-second, and most difficult year. This is a collection of my thoughts throughout, and between, depressive episodes. I am making them public for nothing more than my continued growth.

Acknowledgements

To the reader,
I see you and I love you

To my therapist,
You see me and I love you

1. Fire Reflection

I'm entranced by the flames -two wicks of the candle I lit, thinking only of the scent it would bring- and there is immediate and overwhelming empathy.
They bounce around, fruitlessly doing all they can. Searching, frantically, for more. For any way to escape this little moat of wax that's tauntingly growing. Isolating them from everything they crave. Instead of creating shadows, these tiny flames show a reflection.

I have passing wants, but those are not what I singe for. I lick the air for my needs, dreams, passions, and non-negotiables. But from here, I only see widening and rising wax, and the walls of this jar that I'm burning to break from.
I see a few other flickering wicks, struggling in the melting quicksand of their own wax worlds. I am desperately reaching for them. For the people that understand me. Like-minded individuals to join and burn with. To grow and spread. From meager candles to a forest fire. Natural, formidable, unyielding, and

demanding change. I can see their light, yet I am
seemingly alone.

I need more than what is attainable here, but my wick is
short. My dependence on a breeze-blown curtain to
catch and pull me out is becoming laughably desperate.
For now, I offer what I have; my light, heat and smoke.
All I can hope for is to spark another. To be witnessed
that I am trying. To know that there are other, stronger,
flames that can achieve more. However, when I am
snuffed, I fear I'll be re-lit and nothing will have changed.

2. Rain Will Always Drop

I am 4 and my eyes follow a droplet as it creates a scribbled, vertical clearing. The outside world peeks through a quarter-inch wide path. Someone bigger could easily broaden my sight and wipe the window clean. Instead, my eyes dart to predict the next jagged turn the drop will take.

I am 14 and I "haaaaa" all over the window. I create my own fog to draw and write in. My brother wipes it all away. Hes impatiently watching for any sign of sunlight to play outside. But I only note how easily my thoughts and work are dismissed.

I am 24. I turn the windshield wipers on full blast as soon as I see the first two droplets race to the bottom of the window. I preventatively turn my defrosters on. I have no patience for anything limiting my view.

I am 34 and I hear the twinkling of the rain before I see it. I don't want to just witness it through glass so I grab my boots and walk out the door. It feels so fresh and light that I forget the stresses I left inside. I smile, watching it all, from clouds to puddles and realize I'm 4 again.

3. Breath-Hunting

We've been at it for months. Head down, nose to the grindstone, all work no play. And I need fresh air. Space...

So I take a deep breath, and plan a camping trip.

We set up the tent and set off on a hike. I glance up to see a deer across the canyon, gracefully walking the ridgeline...

I freeze, hold my breath, and watch as she slinks away. We continue toiling on this backcountry trail so forgotten, it's being taken back by nature.

This path of earthy tendrils and spiky inhabitants is steep and riddled with fallen giants we need to climb over...

We're so tired and out of breath, we can only mouth the words "lunch?". We empty our packs into a picnic-pile,

chat, and eat as the sweat stops pouring.
We look around, take stock of how far we've come, and sit in awe of our phenomenal setting...

The vista takes my breath away in its still, silent beauty. Just as I catch it again, lunch is over and we're heading back.
Our boots shuffle in the dirt...

I get back into the rhythm of being winded. My eyes go from ground to sky; darting to see everything. Taking in birds, bugs, clouds, rocks, plants. And before I know it, I see the tent...

The weekend is spent inhaling and exhaling and nothing more. The forest is so pure and free and comfortable. Though I've never been to these woods, I feel at-home and more myself here...

I breathe in and hold onto that wild, earthy air for as long as I can, before my chest insists on pushing it out. I'm already missing it as we At home, we unpack, shower and sink into bed. I feel refreshed, relaxed and ready for life. As I get back to routines and responsibilities, the air becomes stale and stifled again. I picture the trail. The fox. The easy feeling of being...

And I look forward to the day I breathe in deep that fresh mountain air again.

4. Lovely and Lost

I am perpetually in love with getting lost. Be it on some back road, in a book, in a bustling city, or the small details of daily chores. I have always hated the monotonous and rejected routine. I thrive on rolling with the punches and getting to where I need to (or shouldn't) be on my own time. I relentlessly fall in love with hidden gems and the feeling of being somewhere no one has ever been. Leaving my mark in fresh snow or smooth sand that, in my mind, has never been stepped on. Or picking up a fallen leaf that, until today, has been way up on a branch, out of everyone's reach. Or being the first to witness a certain plant bloom, or a butterfly who's only been observed as a caterpillar before.
I hope I will always search for those moments of getting lost, and revel in the thought that there is so much to explore. It sounds silly and childish, and it probably is. Nevertheless, it makes my heart happy.

5. Disappointing Descendant

We take medication to get through the day, and schedule gym time to get into shape.
Play video games til it's 3 in the morning and eat processed food that should come with a warning.

We text on our phones while hitting a vape. Ladies can't leave home without pepper-spray. The Ozone has holes and the whole world is warming. So much access to info, it's no longer informing.

There's trash in the water and it pours acid rain. We complain about wifi while flying on planes. Drive too fast in cars with nowhere to be, and scroll TikTok for hours blaming ADHD.

We use single-use plastic that never breaks down. We praise democracy while bestowing crowns. Use chemicals despite knowingly causing disease. We mourn extinctions while chopping down trees.

Motivated by money, power and praise. We destroy and ignore and reject natural ways. I'm mortified to be a human in these troubled days. What the hell would our ancestors say?

They strived and suffered and fought to survive. What they struggled to earn, our world now deprives. Their land and culture and honor are gone. The grief and heartache they'd feel would be strong.

There's violence and ignorance 24/7. The hatred on Earth now is felt from the heavens. I'm just a descendant and live here for now. I'm trying to focus on making Them proud.

6. All my love, Mama

My mom is a *lot*. She's boisterous, clever, opinionated, blunt, shameless, unwilling to make herself small or quiet for the comfort of others.

She has been everything. A student, a writer, a graduate, a cancer survivor, an example, a reader, the life of the party, a designated driver, an employee of 3 jobs at a time, a volunteer, a widow, a creator, a goofball, a strict authoritarian, a rulebreaker, a representative, a traveler, a leader, a victim, a neighbor, a chauffeur, a cheerleader, a teacher, a maid, a cook, a party planner, a counselor, a decorator, a friend, a girlfriend, a daughter, a sister, an aunt, a mother-in-law and a single mom. I've seen her in so many lights and she truly shines in them all. A kaleidoscopic suncatcher of a Renaissance woman.

She is everything to me. Everything I've ever wanted to be if I ever grew up. The voice in my head, the person who knows me best, THE parent of 3 children (plus some stragglers), my biggest supporter, my debate team, the reason I'm alive, and the reason I'm not dead- those are very different. My friend, my punching bag, the person who holds me accountable, the one person I expect complete honesty from, my secret weapon, and my home.

She's taught me everything I value. To read and drive and get outside. To be picky with friends and boys, but to fiercely give love and loyalty to those I choose. To have a good sense of humor, adventure, and right & wrong. The importance of travel and a good work ethic. The power of a balanced life and colorful meals. To blow out the candles when I'm anxious. To shower and get fresh air when I'm depressed. To stand up straight when I'm self conscious. To drink water after a good cry. And that family loves each other and helps each other. To live a full life before creating another. To bite your nails instead of your tongue. To argue savagely and stubbornly for what you believe in. To cook and swear and prioritize yourself. To be codependent and call it hyper-independence. To question everything, especially authority. To pick your battles and to budget. That anything is possible and everything is survivable.

She gives everything . Love, security, standards, advice, support, a voice, pep talks, scoldings, her whole identity. I am just one of many she has shaped. I am so grateful for everything she is, does and teaches. And yea, it's a *lot*.

7. Homecoming

I eat whole foods and take in as much natural beauty as I can, so that one day, I might be healthy and deserving enough to provide for her.

For the soil that pushes up against my feet and squelches between my toes. I hope she pulls me in and embraces my tired bones.

For the water that cleanses and hydrates me. I ask that she carry my nutrients to necessitous roots.

For the sun that plants freckles on my skin and warms my inner child. I would be honored if she would bleach my bones.

For the mushrooms I scavenge, study, and consume. I implore they reciprocate the sentiment.

For the scent that the flowers emit and the honey which the bees produce. I pray my essence can contribute to their sweetness.

Because I will have returned home to the Earth and she will utilize my vessel to restore herself. Lest I disappoint, deprive, or destroy her like so much of my species..

8. Stop Hitting Yourself

Humans are a short-sighted, hypocritical, ignorant breed

We pump our food full of poison, and prioritize covience over health. Then beg for cures to diseases.

Dedicate entire lives to training for battle and the creation of weapons, just to plead for peace.

Follow leaders and media outlets that promote hate and violence, and then pray for victims.

"Like" posts of people helping others, while averting our eyes during actionable opportunities to do so.

Poach, pollute, and overconsume. Then cry for the polar bears and rhinos and bees.

Think that raping the Earth of petroleum to create unrecycleable, single-use plastic, is more convenient than washing a reusable fork.

Bastardize "green", "hippie", "treehugger", "radical" "idealists" for caring about our health and the health of the planet.

We raise livestock and grow crops for nourishment, and then the Earth farms us. She provides us everything we could ever need and when we die, she ingests us.

Despite knowing this, we spend our entire lives actively hurting ourselves and destroying her. Then have the nerve to question why she's getting heated, sick, and needy now.

It's all the handmade, DIY, self-inflicted, product of our own demise, where we are the bully- and the bullied- in a millenia-long "Stop Hitting Yourself" scene.

9. Discomfort

Life, and everything worth anything is painful.

The physiology of being a human, in and of itself, is excruciating. Growing life and bringing it into the world is unimaginably painful. Then the monotonous pain-tolerance testing begins. Hunger, dehydration, gas, constipation, immune system-building, teething, growth spurts, allergies, disabilities, hormonal changes of puberty/menstrual cycles/menopause, indigestion, exhaustion, normal scrapes/cuts/bruises/headaches/stubbed toes, arthritis, bone fragility, dementia, accidents, medication side effects, genetic issues, exposure risks, dietary constraints. The standard human life is about 73 years of overcoming daily pain.

Physical strength is an obvious benefit of "pushing through the pain". We all know that breathlessness, sweat, and soreness are the price we pay to feel strong. Just finding the motivation, and setting aside the time, to challenge your body's limits is difficult. Let alone literally tearing and repairing your muscles to grow them. Becoming stronger and faster has been a priority for human evolution for thousands of years and will always be worth the sacrifice.

Love is another one of humans' agonizing desires. Loving, and being loved, is the pinnacle of life. But with every love, comes loss, disappointment, heartbreak, and compromise. None of which feel like the gooey, sweet, warmth that love is. We know as individuals, and as a society, that love hurts. We learn it as children through Disney movies. It's reinforced through every song belted, book read, TV channel surfed, and relationship held. But that doesn't stop us.

Wisdom and knowledge goals we all seek; Everyone respects those who know their shit. But being intelligent and experienced comes from being confused and frustrated. It comes from real world experience and learning the hard way. Knowing something ALWAYS stems from not knowing it, and not knowing is uncomfortable. Even the act of learning is tough: Staying up late and skipping parties to study is renowned for being the difficult choice. It's not fun, popular, or satisfying. The state of knowing can also be hard; trying to relay information, or explain, to the willfully ignorant can make anyone wince. And once you know something, you can't un-know it. The cliché "ignorance is bliss" is widespread for a reason.

Happiness is a tricky thing. Everyone has trauma, emotional baggage, and obstacles to achieving mental health. Therapy is notoriously uncomfortable. You dig for the roots of your hardest moments, sit in them, and try to understand how to move forward from them to work through all of it. Choosing to be happy after life throws you curveballs takes mental fortitude that is hard to articulate and even harder to practice. Happy moments are sprinkled into life, but happy people work for that shit.

It's impossible to see the best in people if you can't also acknowledge the bad.
You can't be resilient without strife. You can't be cultured without leaving familiarity. You cannot be forgiving without being mistreated. There is no truth without lies. And there cannot be kindness without cruelty. Life is awful and vicious and uncontrollable, yet magically beautiful. We use the worst bits to become better; stronger, smarter, kinder and more connected, and eventually, those become the best bits.

10. Little Lives

We're all just little kids playing outside.
Oblivious to just how small we are and how quickly the day goes by.
We're all making forts and deciding who we allow in.
Making up the rules as we play the game.

Some of us stroll carelessly, while some stomp with arms crossed.
Some hobble with a pebbles in their shoes but never stop to take them out.
Most of us have watched the lucky ones with rollerskates zoom down the block.
There are bullies who trip kids, and babysitters that carry them.

We get disoriented rolling down grassy hills. We race, looking over our shoulder and get splinters helping friends hop fences. We get distracted, chasing butterflies and our crushes. We walk barefoot on sharp gravel to recover the ball that rolled too far. We seesaw, sitting impossibly high- and then slam down a little too fast. We surprise ourselves by getting through endless, scary tunnels we wanted to explore.

All over the world, we hopscotch one square at a time. In forests, deserts, and snow. In remote villages and cramped cities. On mountaintops and islands.

We find treasures, stub toes, lollygag, skip, hold hands, skin knees, and get on each other's nerves. We all end up bruised, sunburned, filthy and exhausted by dusk. Our paths, pals and processes are so varied and ever-changing. But we all go to bed with wonderment for tomorrow.

11. Familial Lessons

- To meet, raise, and set high standards & hard boundaries - my mom
- Chasing dreams is as easy as buying a ticket - my husband
- Loyalty and pride - my youngest brother
- The power of silence - my oldest brother
- To laugh at myself and life - my Dad
- How good posture and eye contact can seem like confidence - a best friend
- Funny and smart go hand in hand - my cousin
- Weird zoomies and going outside are cool- my dogs
- Good music and shitty beer are all it takes to have a great night- a best friend
- Self improvement and gentleness - my Fairy Grandmother
- Brutal honesty and unquestioning support- a best friend
- Even the most broken things are salvageable - Grandma
- Resilience, resourcefulness, and creativity- (generally

growing up poor, and reminded by) a layoff
- How to use my words, breath and support system - therapy
- To be there for loved ones - my father
- How to forgive - ex boyfriends
- How to forget - depression

12. Sum of My Parts

On my worst day, I am a natural, wildly perfect conundrum.
I am dirty, calloused feet.
I'm sanitized hands.
I am slow meals and fast drives.
Prickly legs.
A soft giggle.
I am freckled cheeks.
A pimple on a chin.
Frizzy hair under a ballcap.
Chipped nailpolish over bitten nails.
Slouched posture.
Straightforward words.
I'm belly rolls and belly-laughs.
Wide hips.
Broad shoulders.
I'm tattoos. Bruises. Mosquito bites.
Uneven tan lines and a shaky voice.
Furrowed brows.
A crooked grin.

Cellulite. Wrinkles. Birthmarks.
Thick hair and thin patience.
I am sweaty armpits.
Dry skin.
Rolling, blue eyes.
Jiggly thighs.
I'm a nose in a book.
A head on a swivel.
A ticklish neck.
Shoulders creeping up to ears.
Gritted teeth and loose lips.
I'm a hot temper.
Cold toes.
Cracked knuckles.
A wandering mind.

I am a full heart.

13. She's Doing It

She felt alone and left home.
She trusted the untrustworthy.
She faced impossible decisions.
She hated her past and sacrificed her future.
She made irresponsible choices.
She didn't know who she was or wanted to be.
She became responsible for two lives.
She grew up alongside her baby.
She was navigating millions of "firsts" while her child did the same.
She's haunted by her childhood.
She's been a mom for her entire adult life.
She never had the examples she set.
She knew what to teach despite never being taught.
She broke generational curses her children never had to see.
She gave trust and support she never received.
She's never faltered in her fearlessness, and never takes herself too seriously.

She did everything for her children.
She's learning to do it for her.

14. Far From It All

I can't remember the last time I was happy for more than half an hour.
I know I've been a happy person.
I know happiness wasn't always fleeting, stolen, or tainted.
I know I've had fun and family and closeness.
I've enjoyed who I was and who was with me.
I know that I once had the ability to be in the moment.
I don't know when I lost that.
Through trauma? Growing up? Seeing the world and who I actually share it with?
Regardless, happiness is slippery for me now.
The constant hunt for it is monotonous.
Now, every day is exhausting.
Each minute takes everything in me.
The only energy I maintain is spent making others comfortable or laugh.
Even with specialized assistance, I just can't seem to conjure what I need.

Where I'm standing feels so seperate from everyone I've loved.
I'm so far from the person I, my parents, brothers, teachers, coaches and friends thought I could be.
I'm lightyears from every good memory I've made.
It's impossible for me to even visualize a happy future.
My brain, the trajectory of my life, and the state of the world don't offer sustainable happiness.
I'm here. Stuck between a fading past and a future so ominously up in the air.

15. Leaving

When I leave this world,
I want to be able to say I saw quite a bit of it
I want to think "I really got to know her"
I want to know I did what I could for her
I want to leave her demanding more friends like me
I want to be proud
I don't want to worry for her
I want to be ready to leave
Not eager, just ready

16. Defensive Nature

Oceans push and pull and spit and drown.
Deserts parch and sting and poke.
Forests suffocate and isolate.
Mountains thin the air and look down in condescension.
And it's all fair because they don't realize I'm unlike my fellow man.
Despite their defensive nature, I do my best to do my best for them.
Because my best is due to them.

17. Known

The rough hands of the man I love intertwined in mine.
Slipping into my weathered hiking boots after a season off.
Calling my best friend crying and hanging up laughing.
The rhythm of tail wags when I open the door.
My brother's subtle inside jokes and perfectly-timed side eye.
The smell of dead leaves and campfire in October.
Settling into my Mom's hug.
The first bite of LJs buffalo chicken pizza after a few years of being away.
The feel of sand, grass, water or a sideview mirror against my bare feet
The sound of mourning doves settling everyone down for the evening

The Universe nudges and nods to remind me that I still fit here. Saying "I know you better than you remember yourself. This Dani-shaped place in life is still right here. Remember?".

18. Neuro Conquistador

At war with my brain
Keeping the enemy too close
And friends much too far
Antidepressant grenades attack isolation and lethargy
Therapy hostage negotiations easing negative self talk
The acronym faceoff: TMS combat ADHD
Ketamine up against anxiety
It's back and forth,
Touch and go,
Guerilla warfare
I am alone,
Behind enemy lines
I'm losing

19. Waiting For

Time
Change
Support
Direction
Motivation
Being ready
The right time
Empty promises
Feeling deserving
Prior priorities
A companion
Permission
Inspiration
Perfection
Comfort
Savings
Energy

20. In 28C and My Head

Its 1:30 PM as I take off.
It feels like I'm betraying everyone. I'm leaving everyone I love.
Leaving everything I've ever accumulated, aside from my one checked bag somewhere beneath me. I've felt the necessity and pull of this for years.
I expected to feel excitement. Success or freedom? I'm not sure.

But I just feel deep-seeded, irrefutable ***guilt.***
For letting everyone and thing in my life stay when I know they'd be better off leaving as well. For not being able to just be content with life here.
For leaving loved ones to mop up the life and home I built here.
For my decision forcing some to choose between staying or coming.
For knowing my leaving would hurt those, and doing it anyway.
For leaving my animals, temporarily; not knowing why I

left.

For everyone who doesn't understand why I needed to leave.

For those I didn't get to say goodbye to.

For the hurt and worry I cause.

For prioritizing my needs in general.

For wanting too much.

I feel cavernous ***sadness.***

For feeling safer going somewhere I've never been, alone, than to stay home surrounded by everyone and thing I love.

For finality of knowing I'll probably never return to live in here again;

And therefore committing to short-term visits with everyone here for the rest of my life.

For never having felt at home here.

For not knowing if I'll ever feel it anywhere.

For the doubt that anyone will want to join me. For the loneliness and sadness I, and they, feel. For feeling like I made the wrong choice.

For feeling I made the right one.

For knowing a lot of people will be judging me for this.

For the uncertainty of my future.

For not wanting to stay, and not wanting to leave.

I feel a lifetime's worth of ***anger***

For everyone being shocked by my leaping at an opportunity.
For them assuming I wouldn't actually leave, despite me openly yearning to this whole time. For the pushback and judgment.
At the requests to postpone my needs and dreams even longer- all the way up to my takeoff.
For having let myself fall in step with everyone else's timelines and priorities.
For having stayed too long.
For feeling desperate and jumping at the first opportunity.
For being alone on this plane.
For allowing my setting and circumstances to almost end me.
At my country's continued & dangerous ignorance.
At myself for feeling sad and guilty in this moment.
At loved ones stringing me along with no intention of ever supporting these needs or feelings.
For the fact that I let them.
At the lack of acknowledgement and encouragement to be doing a difficult thing.
At the emphasis of me "running away, as opposed to mygenuie excitement to "run toward".
For feeling questioned and judged instead to supported and cheered.
Regardless, I'm in seat 28C.

Alone, emotional and terrified.
I would rather these feelings haunt me forever, than spend another second as that ghost of myself.

www.ingramcontent.com/pod-product-compliance
Lightning Source LLC
Chambersburg PA
CBHW070039070426
42449CB00012BA/3095